MINKS

WILD ANIMALS OF THE WOODS

Lynn M. Stone

The Rourke Press, Inc.
Vero Beach, Florida 32964

PHOTO CREDITS
© Tom and Pat Leeson: page 8; © Tom Ulrich: pages 10, 13;
© Lynn M. Stone: cover, title page, pages 4, 7, 15, 17, 18, 21

Library of Congress Cataloging-in-Publication Data

Stone, Lynn M.
    Minks / Lynn Stone.
        p. cm. — (Wild Animals of the woods)
    Includes index.
    ISBN 1-57103-095-6
    1. Minks—North America—Juvenile literature.
[1. Minks.]   I. Title II. Series: Stone, Lynn M.   Wild Animals of the
woods.
QL737.C25S74 1995
599.74' 447—dc20   94–46896
                                                          CIP
                                                          AC

Printed in the USA

TABLE OF CONTENTS

MINKS

The mink perhaps should have been called "water weasel." The sleek, quick mink is a close cousin of weasels. But unlike the slightly smaller weasels, the mink loves to swim and prowl stream banks.

The person who comes upon a wild mink may see only a brown blur. Minks always seem to be in motion—running, swimming, diving and sniffing.

Mink hunt in and around streams and ponds

HOW THEY LOOK

The soft, rich fur of wild minks is usually dark brown. Now and then, a mink has scattered patches of white, usually on its underside.

Like weasels and river otters, minks have rather long bodies and short legs. A large wild mink may weigh three pounds and stretch 24 inches from its nose to the tip of its tail.

Mink wear soft, thick coats of dark fur

WHERE THEY LIVE

Minks live in Alaska, Canada and most of the lower 48 states. They are not found in the Far North of Canada or in the desert areas of the Southwest.

Minks like dense plant cover along streams, ponds, rivers and marshes. Minks are small enough to dart into openings among roots and under stones.

Minks sometimes dig burrows just above the water's edge. A mink may take over a muskrat lodge for its own home.

A mink may take over a muskrat's home after killing the muskrat, as this mink has done

HOW THEY ACT

Minks are active throughout the seasons, except in the coldest weather. But minks lead very secret lives, partly because they are largely **nocturnal** (nahk TUR nul)—active at night.

Adult minks, especially males, travel alone. A male mink may travel several miles looking for food.

The hunt often takes the mink into a brook or pond. A mink can dive as deep as 18 feet and swim about 90 feet under water.

*Mink stay active throughout
the seasons*

The mink's cousin, the river otter, is larger and more at home in water

A mink hustles over ice to a pool of open water

PREDATOR AND PREY

Underwater, a hunting mink looks for fish, crayfish or even a muskrat. A muskrat can outweigh a mink, but it can't outswim a mink or dodge its sharp teeth.

Minks hunt along shorelines for **prey** (PRAY), such as frogs, insects, worms and nesting birds.

Sometimes the mink slips off to a meadow to hunt mice or rabbits. Meanwhile, the mink itself has to watch out for **predators** (PRED uh tors)—foxes, dogs, owls and coyotes.

14   *A mink munches on a small bass*

MINK BABIES

A mother mink bears a litter of two to ten babies in spring. They are born in a cozy, underground nest lined with fur and feathers from the mother's prey.

Newborn mink are helpless. Their eyes open at five weeks. Soon afterward they begin to hunt with their mother.

By autumn the young minks are nearly full-grown, and they separate from their mother.

A young mink begins to explore its watery world in a marsh

THE MINK'S COUSINS

The mink is one of the meat-eating animals that scientists call mustelids. Most mustelids produce strong scents from their body's **musk** (MUHSK) glands. Minks produce a strong scent, but it is not as powerful as a skunk's.

Other North American mustelids include otters, fishers, martens, black-footed ferrets, badgers, weasels and wolverines.

Mustelids live in many different **habitats** (HAB uh tats), or surroundings. Otters spend most of their time in water. Badgers live in grassland burrows and martens hunt the treetops.

Minks produce a strong, musky scent, but it isn't as powerful as the skunk's

MINKS AND PEOPLE

Among the members of the weasel family, skunks are known for their odor. Minks are known for their fur.

Mink fur is valuable to furriers, people who make coats from mink **pelts** (PELTS), as the skin and fur is called. A mink coat can be worth $15,000.

Most pelts used in coats are from large, farm-raised minks. Each coat requires from 25 to 70 pelts.

Trappers sell the rich fur of minks for use in coats

THE MINK'S FUTURE

About 1880, the sea mink became **extinct** (ex TINKT). That's not likely to happen with the mink. Minks are fairly common throughout the habitats in which they live. Trappers still take several thousand minks for their fur each winter.

In a few locations, however, mink have disappeared. That is because they have eaten fish poisoned by pollution or had their habitat destroyed.

Glossary

extinct (ex TINKT) — having disappeared completely; no longer existing

habitat (HAB uh tat) — the kind of place in which an animal lives, such as woodland

musk (MUHSK) — a strong-smelling liquid made by certain animals, such as mink and other mustelids

nocturnal (nahk TUR nul) — active at night

pelt (PELT) — the skin and fur of a mammal

predator (PRED uh tor) — an animal that kills other animals for food

prey (PRAY) — an animal that is hunted by another for food

INDEX